Designing a Happier Life

Feng Shui with Lurrae

A Guidebook

Lurrae Lupone

Dedication

With gratitude to friends and teachers
who have crossed my path
"for a reason, a season, or a lifetime"
on the transformational journey of my life.

In Appreciation

Book Design: Halagan Design Group www.halagandesign.com
Line Drawings by Melodie Provenzano www.melodieprovenzano.com
Edited by Lara Asher

ISBN 978-0-9899851-0-9

The purpose of Feng Shui is
to deflect ill fortune,
to attract good luck,
and to create the blessings
of health, harmony, and prosperity
by influencing our destiny through
the cultivation of chi

–Chinese Proverb

Contents

Foreword vi

I-Understanding Feng Shui.....................1

Explaining Historical Origins 2
The Bagua 10
Evolution of the Eight Trigrams, the Pa'kua, and Bagua 11
Introducing the Feng Shui Guidebook 12
Designing Your Life 16

II-The Feng Shui Conversation............. 21

Beginning Our Conversation 22
Setting Priorities for Your Life Goals and Aspirations 24
Your Personal Profile of the Nine Life Aspirations 25
Flourishing in Your Life 26
Clarifying Life Goals 28
The Bagua 29
Locating Your New Placements 30
Evaluating Landscape Features 32
Having Fun with Chinese Astrology 34
 Your Feng Shui Astrology...36

III-The Feng Shui Consultation............. 39

Honoring Your Process with Feng Shui 40
Reviewing Key Placements 42
The Aspects of the Bagua 44

Evaluating Your Property, Home, Bedroom, Children's
Bedrooms, Home Office Kitchen, and Living Room
Through Feng Shui Eyes 47

Taking Time to Summarize Corrections 60

IV–Taking Action to Create a Happier Life 63

Taking Action with Feng Shui 64

Designing Your Own Remedies and Solutions 65

Choosing to Change Your Life 66

Designing the Ceremony 68

Sequence for Designing Your Ceremonial Activations 69

The Red Envelope Tradition 70

Fees, Referrals, and Testimonials 71

Sharing Feng Shui Stories 72

Having Fun with Feng Shui 74

Enjoying Life's Journey 75

Concluding Thoughts 76

Manifesting Happiness and Flow 77

Defining Feng Shui Terms 78

References 80

In Gratitude 81

About the Author 82

Foreword

Finding happiness is a human pursuit, sometimes illusive, yet when present, happiness is hard to contain. It is reflected by an inner glow or smile, spreading like sunshine to others. Like everything in nature, we cycle through many different states of being and moods. Inevitably you experience the entire spectrum of human emotions from fear, grief, sadness, depression, feeling OK or fine, to laughter, happiness, perhaps exaltation, and ecstasy.

Life begins with a cry, but in a short time a baby is smiling; the inner wellspring of the life force energy and happiness emerge. Children embody playfulness and pure joy. At some point, self-awareness, conscious intent, and a motivation to explore and pursue interests, dreams, and a life of happiness activate. Meaningful accomplishments move us toward a feeling of success and possibly recognition or fame. Ideally, you reach your highest potential with your unique gifts and talents. Some do so despite what might seem like incredible circumstances. Some offer their talents and gifts not only for wealth or personal reasons but also for the good of community or mankind.

Science has proven success is not the result of happiness, but rather, happiness contributes to success. You can affect your happiness quotient by developing certain habits throughout your day and over your lifetime. Feeling the effervescence of laughter, happiness and joy, satisfaction from meaningful work, and stillness from within is attainable, so that "when you smile, the whole world will smile with you."

I suggest one of the ways to begin to design a happier life is to consider your home environments as the template. Try launching your happier life and transformation by implementing the common sense principles of the 5,000-year-old Chinese ancient art and science of Feng Shui. I offer my Feng Shui Consultation Guidebook as a method for you to begin by using your own sacred spaces. I hope you find this guidebook helpful on your journey to a happier life.

1-Understanding Feng Shui

We begin with a historical background to understand the ancient Chinese 5,000-year-old environmental science, the art of placement and design, known as Feng Shui to:

- Receive a frame of reference for its origins, based on centuries of observation of the landscape and how environments empower happiness and success

- Visualize the ideal home site created by the four mystical animals of Tortoise, Dragon, Tiger, and Phoenix

- Honor the ancient Book of Changes, the *I Ching*, and the sages who contributed to its development as an oracle

- Grasp concepts of the flexible Bagua template, The Nine Life Aspirations, and different schools of Feng Shui

- Prepare to engage the teachings and tools of Feng Shui to move toward health, happiness, and prosperity for yourself

"Feng Shui is the ecology of flow, the architecture of energy.

Based on the idea that good fortune results when people live in balance with their environments and their inner natures.

Feng Shui has been praised as an environmentally sound practice that emphasizes respecting rather than tampering with nature.

Today, this ancient and intuitive idea is so forgotten as to seem revolutionary."

– Elizabeth Miles

Explaining Historical Origins

Feng Shui is the ancient Chinese art and science of healing spaces. It is based on Taoist philosophy, common sense, and centuries of observation and accumulated wisdom of how happy, healthy, and successful people benefited from the landscape and environmental design of their original home sites.

It is based on the belief that man has the potential to experience health and vitality, happiness and balance, and ultimately, success and prosperity. But how? By living in a home built in a complete shape of harmonic design on an ideal home site. Here he can optimize the benefits of the vital life force energy coming from his environment known as chi. He will prosper best in a place with clean, fresh air to breathe; bright sunshine to liven his spirit and foster the growth of healthy crops; fresh water to drink and supply his crops; and protection from harsh north winds.

The choices for finding this ideal home site may have been easier to achieve in years past, but the same essential principles still apply in modern times. Feng Shui principles of how man is connected to his environment are part of the recent revival of 5,000 years of Chinese civilization and culture, exemplified in the extraordinary worldwide performances of "ShenYun2013.com," which celebrate the cultural heritage and beautiful landscape of China.

The words *Feng* and *Shui* literally mean "wind" and "water" and are pronounced "fung schway." These two words come from observations of how wind and water energies circulated on earth and how people learned to benefit from those energies. The term Feng Shui is derived from the ancient poem below created to describe the ideal landscape for a home site, emphasizing the power of environments to affect human life and success. Imagine what this home site would look and feel like. Does it reflect your home site?

> The wind is mild, the sun shines,
> the water is clear, the vegetation lush

Early man recognized and honored the interdependence and connectedness between himself and his immediate landscape, with the earth below and the heavenly forces above. The position of his home had everything to do with safety, survival, and his potential prosperity. He sought a home site where his crops would thrive.

Feng Shui has become part of the common vernacular. If not understood in its entirety, many people understand that it has something to do with how our surroundings affect us, such as where you place the bed, decorating to improve the energy, not having a tree or pole blocking your front door, or that placing your desk in the commanding position facing the door can lead to success.

Early Feng Shui masters known as Geomancers—"geo" means earth; "mancy" means the divination or messages from the earth—interpreted the features and qualities of the landscape to determine the most auspicious gravesite or home site. They translated the energy of the landscape and reported natural events to the emperor, such as the exact date of spring's arrival when they observed a feather had risen from the earth to the top of a bamboo stick.

Geomancers studied landscape features, such as mountains, hills, fertile valleys, water features, and distant views in search of the classical ideal home site shape that would offer comfort, protection, and prosperity known as "the arm chair effect."

Four mystical animals—Tortoise, Dragon, Tiger, and Phoenix—symbolize this idealized site. The Tortoise is symbolic of a protective north mountain sitting behind the house, the Dragon's hills (yang-male) rest on the west side, and the Tiger's gentler hills (yin-female) sit on the east side. The home itself would sit safely halfway up the mountain, facing south. The home has a water feature in front to nourish the crops and faces a wide and distant view (ming tang), symbolized by the Phoenix, offering the prospect of unlimited opportunities coming from all directions. However, the fundamental concept underlying all analysis was about capturing the beneficial flow of *sheng chi*, known as the vital life force energy and the cosmic breath.

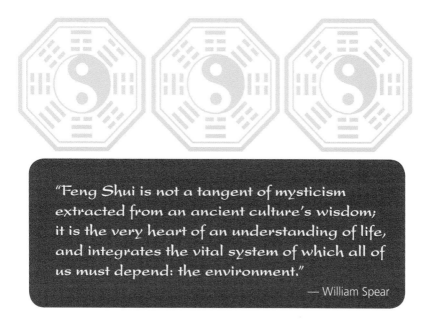

> "Feng Shui is not a tangent of mysticism extracted from an ancient culture's wisdom; it is the very heart of an understanding of life, and integrates the vital system of which all of us must depend: the environment."
> — William Spear

To understand Feng Shui, you must begin with the revered sacred and mystical text of Chinese thought known as the *I Ching*, or *Book of Changes*, written over centuries by such sages as Confucius and Lao Tzu. Considered the mother of Chinese philosophy, it is used as an oracle to understand and solve life problems and challenges on a higher spiritual level. The core principle of the *I Ching* is that life is constantly changing, and the laws of nature are also the laws of humanity. Since nature and humanity are one, harmony is the key to life. The Way of the Universe is expressed by the symbol of the Tao, with the movement of yin and yang, the energy principle of opposing forces, ever changing, one into the other, yet both balancing and attracting, such as female and male, soft and hard, winter and summer, cold and hot, night and day.

In the *I Ching*, yin, the female energy, is expressed as three divided lines, and yang, the male energy, as three solid lines. These three lines, combinations of either yin or yang lines, are known as *trigrams,* while a combination of two sets of trigrams form a *hexagram* of six lines. The *I Ching* contains the thoughtful system of these sixty-four hexagrams, which combine all permutations of trigrams of yin and yang lines. Each hexagram offers an interpretation and spiritual guidance for all life situations. It is used as an oracle by throwing six sticks or coins that refer to one of the sixty-four hexagrams for interpretation of your fate.

Also taken from the *I Ching* is a symbolic octagonal template known as the Baqua, which depicts the yin yang balancing symbol, the Tao, at its center. Surrounding the Tao symbol are eight trigrams known as Heaven, Earth, Wind, Thunder, Fire, Water, Lake, and Mountain. The philosophical interpretation and use of the Baqua continues in great depth to attributes and qualities of the Five Elements of Fire, Earth, Metal, Water, and Wood and also to another layer known as the Nine Life Aspirations of Wealth & Prosperity, Fame & Reputation, Love & Relationships, Health & Family, Harmony & Balance (The Tao), Children & Creativity, Wisdom & Spirituality, Career & Life Path, Travel & Helpful People, and on and on to many other deeper energetic levels of meaning. However, the simplest metaphor for the depth of meaning attributed to the Baqua is the Magic Square in which all of the above mentioned energies and layers might be synthesized and symbolized by numbers from one to nine. Here, magically, all lines across, down, and diagonally, add up to the sum of fifteen, with the yin yang symbol of the Tao at the center represented by the number five.

**Octagonal Baqua with Tai Chi Symbol
of Yin and Yang Surrounded by the Eight Trigrams**

The Magic Square

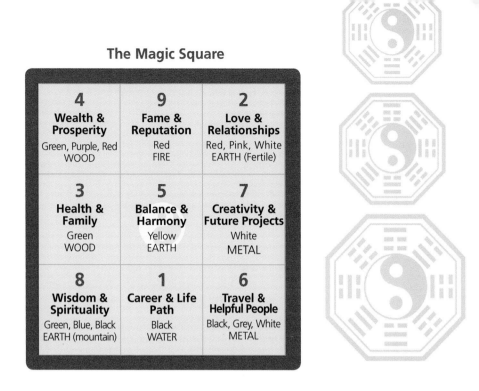

4	9	2
Wealth & Prosperity	**Fame & Reputation**	**Love & Relationships**
Green, Purple, Red WOOD	Red FIRE	Red, Pink, White EARTH (Fertile)
3	**5**	**7**
Health & Family	**Balance & Harmony**	**Creativity & Future Projects**
Green WOOD	Yellow EARTH	White METAL
8	**1**	**6**
Wisdom & Spirituality	**Career & Life Path**	**Travel & Helpful People**
Green, Blue, Black EARTH (mountain)	Black WATER	Black, Grey, White METAL

The Bagua template is the tool used by Feng Shui masters and consultants to identify the quality of the universal energies of your property, home, rooms, and work spaces. It is also used to help you identify which of the Nine Life Aspirations you seek to change and balance in your life and which may be out of balance and causing unhappiness. Much of life is out of your control, but you still can design your life through your intentions and creative ideas, utilizing your home as a metaphor for your desired life. Feng Shui suggests using the spaces of your property and home as the template to create the life you want. Have fun. Just go for it!

There are several schools of thought on Feng Shui, beginning with the Geomancy School, which evolved into the Landscape School, Compass School, Classical School, and the Modern or Contemporary School. The Compass and Classical schools placed an emphasis on the cardinal and intermediate directions as the location of universal energies known as the Five Elements of Fire, Earth, Metal, Water, and Wood. In recent decades, Feng Shui has experienced a growth in popularity, particularly in the West.

This has led to some confusion due to opposing views and schools of thought about the proper orientation of the Bagua over your property and home. If you accept ancient concepts of the power of your environment to affect your life, then how might the template be applied to your property and home site to locate new placements for the life you wish to create?

Whereas the Compass and Classical schools placed the Bagua Energies strictly according to the cardinal directions, the new view from the Contemporary School's perspective of Feng Shui contended two fundamental differences. One, modern man no longer has the ability to select his home site with the same freedom as in the past. Now people live in multiple dwellings, condos, and high rise buildings, which are not always oriented toward the south. Two, an aspect attributed to China that identified Hong Kong as the center of "wealth" located in the Southeast of the country does not necessarily apply in the United States, where the center of wealth might more properly be located with the Stock Exchange on Wall Street in New York City, which is in the Northeast.

The interest and application of Feng Shui principles grew when Master Professor Lin Yun brought the ancient tradition of Tibetan Tantric Buddhism Black Sect Feng Shui to the West in the 1970's. Lin Yun contended the Classical school's emphasis on cardinal and intermediate directions need not apply, but rather, the position of the Bagua was a fluid and moveable concept that could be oriented and overlaid from the ever-changing position of entrance doors as the mouth of chi and the source of cosmic energy. The Bagua was not stationery as when aligned with the cardinal directions but could be moved to where the vital sheng chi entered to nourish the inhabitants — from the driveway as the entrance to the property, to the entrance door of the home, and additionally to the individual doorways of each room. It is from this vantage point and moveable Bagua that I offer my suggestions to balance the chi flow and help you activate your life goals with suggested corrections, solutions, remedies, and reminders. My goal for you is that you experience a new sense of wellbeing and happiness and flourish in ways you never imagined.

Professor Lin Yun's modern perspective on Feng Shui taught another and yet deeper concept regarding the Bagua. The front entrance door to the home was also the doorway that led the way outside, the pathway to one's life's work and career. When you leave from your front door, is your sidewalk clear and smooth? Does it offer a distant view, and therefore a vision where unlimited opportunities come to you from all directions and are possible for you to attain? From this modern orientation, the area of the Bagua known as Career (North, Water) is superimposed over the entrance to the property (driveway) and next, over the front door, and so forth. This is where the energies actually enter the spaces to nourish you and the place from which you go out into the world on your "Life's Journey." It is from this orientation that the other energies of the Bagua of Fire, Earth, Metal, and Wood naturally fall into their respective places, accompanied by the attributes of the Nine Life Aspirations.

The Bagua template is the essential tool used by consultants to suggest placement of "cures and remedies," Feng Shui terminology used to describe suggested corrections to chi flow as well as new placements that become metaphorical expressions for the life you are designing by your new placements and reminders.

I honor all schools and master teachers who have passed on to me this sacred and heretofore secret knowledge, originally transmitted only by oral tradition. I incorporate aspects of all schools in my consultations, but I focus primarily on the Landscape and Contemporary Schools.

I approach my Feng Shui consultations with you from this contemporary orientation of the Bagua energies and offer my suggestions to correct the flow of chi on your property and in your home, so that new placements will help you to actualize your goals. Few people have the luxury of selecting their home site, but you are still able to work with the same universal energies to balance your life, starting from the entrance to your property and to your home from your front door, known as the mouth of chi.

The Bagua

An Octagon Consisting of Eight Trigrams
Symbolizing the Feng Shui Energies of the Universe
from the Perspective of
Tibetan Tantric Buddhism
Black Sect Feng Shui

S

SE

SW

4
**Wealth &
Prosperity**
Green, Purple, Red
WOOD
Early Summer
Thigh
Eldest Daughter
WIND
Sun

9
**Fame &
Reputation**
Red
FIRE
Summer
Eye
Middle Daughter
FIRE
Li

2
**Love &
Relationships**
Red, Pink, White
EARTH
Early Autumn
Internal Organs
Mother/Sister
EARTH
Kun

E

3
**Health &
Family**
Green
WOOD
Spring
Foot
Eldest Son
THUNDER
Chen

5
**Balance &
Harmony**
Yellow
EARTH
Health
Tai Chi

7
**Creativity &
Future Projects**
White
METAL
Late Autumn
Mouth
Youngest Daughter
LAKE
Dui

W

8
**Wisdom &
Spirituality**
Green, Black, Blue
EARTH
Late WInter
Hand
Youngest Son
MOUNTAIN
Ken

1
**Career &
Life's Journey**
Black
WATER
Winter
Ear
Middle Son
WATER
Kan

6
**Travel &
Helpful People**
Black, Gray, White
METAL
Early Winter
Head
Father/Brother
HEAVEN
Chien

NE

N

NW

Evolution of the Eight Trigrams, the Pa'kua, and Bagua

The Bagua consists of eight symbolic trigrams. A trigram is composed of three lines either broken (yin) or solid (yang), originating from records about Chinese King Fu Hsi, who was known as a master of divination. He saw a horse and tortoise rising from Ho River with special markings on their backs, which became known as the Lo-Shu (Magic Square). This explained the Pa'qua of the Earlier Heaven Sequence, depicting eight trigrams as the order of nature in opposing polarities — Heaven and Earth, Wind and Thunder, Water and Fire, Mountain and Lake. The Later Heaven Sequence of the trigrams described the cycles of the four seasons.

During the period of King Wen, further evolutions of the Lo-Shu Pa'kua expanded from eight trigrams to permutations of the eight trigrams known as the sixty-four hexagrams in the *I Ching*.

During the time of Confucius, Feng Shui was used by the imperial court for siting the palace according to astrological calculations best for the Emperor. By the Chin dynasty A.D. 265-420, the practice of Feng Shui as divination had evolved and was recognized by the imperial court as an accepted Taoist practice and used for divining auspicious sites.

Hexagram 20
Kun/Contemplation

Sun Wood 4

Kun Earth 2

By One's Thoughts
One Commands

Today, the Contemporary School of Feng Shui has adapted the Bagua to the environment of the client, rather than aligning with the cardinal directions. Despite confusion regarding the use and evolution of the Bagua, the inherent values of Feng Shui remain as man and humanity continue to be affected by and between the heavenly forces above, the earthly forces below, and within the universal order of all things. And over time, the eight trigrams and the sixty-four hexagrams of the *I Ching have* remained constant — used for divination, spiritual guidance, and embracing the wisdom of the Taoist way, honoring man's vital connection to nature and his environment.

Hexagram 57
Ko/Revolution (Molting)

Dui Metal 7

Li Fire 9

Changes Are
Now Possible

Introducing the Feng Shui Guidebook

The Feng Shui Guidebook is designed to enable you to comprehend basic Feng Shui concepts, my consultation process, record suggestions to correct and cultivate the flow of chi, and encourage speedy action on suggested "cures and remedies" to implement your goals, which will lead to designing a happier life.

Feng Shui with Lurrae is a unique form of life coaching that takes place in the personal spaces of your home and business. It is a different sort of therapeutic experience. It applies harmonic designs with the sacred practice of Feng Shui that respects how the natural world and environments and ancient philosophical concepts affect our lives, happiness, and future success.

Feng Shui with Lurrae seeks to increase and enhance the smooth flow of energy, known as the cosmic breath or sheng chi to interior environments and to neutralize negative energy, sha chi. The intent is to design buildings with harmonic designs to support health, which leads to happiness, harmony, balance, and ultimately to success and prosperity. The primary Feng Shui principle is to enhance human health and vitality by inviting good energy, known as chi, into our interior spaces to achieve the natural benefits of the outdoors — fresh air, oxygen, and sunshine — to where we live, sleep, and work.

Many people appreciate the benefits of Feng Shui but don't know how to begin. This Guidebook may assist you in understanding the essential elements of Feng Shui, my personal perspective, and my

> The power of intuitive understanding will protect you from harm until the end of your days.
>
> — Lao Tzu

format for the Feng Shui consultation process. Spaces are provided for your notes and to record my suggestions, corrections, and remedies. My consultations are designed with an order that is easy to understand, so you will be motivated to take action on my suggestions. My goal is to validate the life you desire, to let go of the past, and inspire and encourage you to implement recommendations by making new placements of furniture, using your most cherished art, objects, belongings, and treasures. I encourage making three new placements with intentions immediately. By making visible changes in your spaces, you will feel empowered, joyful, and realize results more quickly. I encourage follow up questions, conversations, and coaching sessions as life situations are always in a state of flux. Make one change and everything starts to move in the direction you desire.

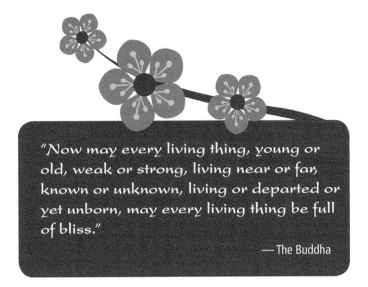

> "Now may every living thing, young or old, weak or strong, living near or far, known or unknown, living or departed or yet unborn, may every living thing be full of bliss."
>
> — The Buddha

There is a Chinese saying which a master flower arranger has the ability to fill up an empty room with just one flower, so deft is the master's art and skill. So, too, the skilled Feng Shui consultant strives to arrange the intangible flow of chi in a place for the benefit of its inhabitants by choosing the most appropriate, out of many possibilities. Similarly, your decision to implement just one new placement with intention will bring you closer to feeling a new sense of happiness that may make everything in your life now seem possible and easy.

Prior to your consultation, I request your birthdate, a copy of the assessors map or property survey showing the shape of your property, a diagram of the house with a footprint showing the shape of the home, and floor plans showing entrance doors, room layouts, and windows to analyze the flow of chi. Hand drawn is fine. I prepare materials which include your Feng Shui astrology, personal trigram, lucky directions, and house numerology. Are you a Fire, Earth, Metal, Water, or Wood element? Knowing what element you are is helpful in suggesting the most beneficial colors for your personal spaces, such as bedroom and office, and colors of clothes you might wear.

The Feng Shui Guidebook is organized as follows: First, I honor the sacred invitation to visit your home for purposes of a Feng Shui consultation; I make calculations based on your birthdate for your astrology, and use a copy of a survey, property, and home shape for preliminary analysis; During *The Feng Shui Conversation*, I listen closely to your needs, wants, and dreams. This process can also be completed over the phone or by Skype. I identify your three most relevant life goals taken from your personal profile of the Nine Life Aspirations of the Bagua, and how features of your exterior and interior landscape influence your chi level and cultivation. I am here to validate your life, bring clarity to your aspirations and passions, and determine areas where you may feel out of balance, unhappy, or unfulfilled. I view this time as vital and as the most important aspect of the consultation. I ascertain your deepest reasons for considering Feng Shui. I believe you already know your spaces are affecting your life and can be improved in some way.

The Feng Shui Consultation continues with my visual evaluation of your exterior and interior landscape, reviewing property, home, and individual rooms from the macro to micro view to analyze even the smallest placements on your desk and tabletops. Here, I offer suggestions for correction of chi flow and then new placements to activate your future goals and intentions. The goal is to cultivate a flow of sheng chi to support health and vitality, harmony and balance, leading to empowerment, prosperity, and happiness. I offer suggestions that may include comments on property shape, building design, and structure; the primary placements of bed, desk, and stove are reviewed for personal empowerment, financial success, and health; placements of furniture, art, and objects; balancing the five elements; and colors most beneficial to you — all to invite energy and emphasis where it is needed at this time.

Feng Shui

wind   water

The Feng Shui Consultation for Business necessarily follows the Conversation and Consultation for Home, as features of your property and home form the foundation for your life and future success.

I offer additional services such as Transcendental Cures and Ceremonies from the perspective of Tibetan Tantric Buddhism Black Sect Feng Shui, House Clearings, Harmonic Designs and Shapes for new house construction, and Teen Shui. I offer Life Coaching Conversations that are also available via phone and Skype. Making changes in personal spaces with intention may trigger dramatic effects on your "inner space," allowing goals to manifest in daily life.

Feng Shui principles are based on 5,000 years of ancient Chinese wisdom, observation, and common sense. The practice of Feng Shui is profound, mystical, and sacred work. Feng Shui with Lurrae is confidential, powerful, and fun.

Designing Your Life

What is the life you wish to design? How do you stay in balance while the speed of change and technology affects every part of your life? The challenge is ever greater to come home to yourself. Maslow's pyramid and hierarchy of needs theorizes that man moves upward from biological and physiological needs, to safety, to belongingness and love, to esteem, to then achieve self-actualization. I suggest that being all you can be includes balancing the yin and yang of our lives not only in homes that support our desired lifestyle and goals but also in peaceful surroundings, a variety of foods to nourish us, and daily exercise — a reminder that the essential role of Feng Shui is about health and vitality. So to, within that natural order, modern man seeks to design his life with meaning and fullfilment in all things.

> "Once you make a decision, the universe conspires to make it happen."
> — Ralph Waldo Emerson

Our lives are shaped within a context of the universal order and circadian rhythms marked by years, seasons, phases of the moon, and days of the week, representing the ever changing ebb and flow of life. I have enjoyed for many years a method to stay in balance with the natural order and cycles of nature with a health and exercise program. This program by Dr. Irving Dardik, the SuperWave principle and LifeWaves, suggests all of life is waves and cycles. This program promotes health and longevity and is designed to balance and synchronize the body with the circadian rhythms of nature through cycles of exercise (yang) and recovery (yin), which increase heart rate variability. LifeWaves is similar to the concept of the Tao, which symbolizes the unification of polar opposites of yin and yang, rest and activity.

This guidebook is intended to act as a simple and easy road map for you to follow and to record my suggestions during *The Feng Shui Consultation*. I have designed the order from the macro view of your property (yang-active) to the micro (yin-quiet) of interior, personal, intimate, and restorative spaces of your home.

The suggested cures and remedies will include corrections of chi flow that utilize your personal treasures and belongings and will be activated with intention and a ceremony. Some solutions may be considered transcendental, illogical, and mystical. However, I tend to suggest creative arrangements of your belongings, seldom suggesting something new other than fresh green plants and flowers. Where appropriate, a traditional Chinese remedy is possible.

Feng Shui with Lurrae is deeply personal and may be therapeutic. As you shift your "inner space" and "heart space," and listen to your inner voice, you gain clarity as your deepest intentions may be realized. Placing and planting favorite things in view become metaphors for your life — your goals as seeds, planting dreams, germinating, reaching full flower of achievement.

Everything changes. I view life as a transformational safari where you adapt and grow from those changes and challenges. We want to live an honest, authentic, purposeful life and find our calling, bliss, and joy. Home is a sacred space that offers a safe place to work out those challenges, and, like the phases of the moon, we can cycle from darkness to light.

Feng Shui with Lurrae begins with *The Feng Shui Conversation* to validate, listen, and learn what you desire to create in life. Next, in *The Feng Shui Consultation*, I review your exterior and interior landscape for beneficial chi flow, followed by suggested corrections, to manifest the life goals you desire. I believe we are attracted to a property and home as a karmic workshop to meet the next challenges on the path of life we are designing or have chosen to follow. Even though everything changes, every life is presented with

great challenges. What we least expect, and can never imagine, happens. Our homes as sacred space offer an opportunity to put our goals before us, as we let go of the past and endeavor to meet those challenges.

The power of Feng Shui begins with clarity and clearings and takes shape when activating new placements of furniture and belongings with intention. We then anchor and seal them with a ceremony in specific areas of the Bagua. Our intention attracts new energy just as an acupuncturist places a needle to direct the flow of chi along meridians to heal the body.

The Chinese have a concept of sying and yi. Sying is the physical, tangible, observable world. Yi is the intangible, unobservable, transcendental world. The power of Feng Shui is reached when we set intentional goals with new placements, sying, then create a ceremony, thereby anchoring our deepest intentions with the intangible, transcendental, mystical, yi.

Feng Shui can transform your life and move you toward future goals. Your spaces are sacred and act as a metaphor for who you are. You can create spaces that reflect who you want to become. You have everything you need. Feng Shui helps you put things in the right place. Delight in using cherished belongings. Imbue them with new meaning, intention, and power.

What you see is what you get.
More happiness awaits.
Let's begin. . . .

Ask, and you will receive; seek, and you will find;
knock, and the door will be opened to you.

— Matthew 7:7-11

II–The Feng Shui Conversation

We begin with the Feng Shui Conversation so that I may better understand who you are and what you hope to achieve through your Feng Shui experience. I promise to:

- Be with you and listen closely

- Hear what you say you really want in life and what is missing

- Get a sense of who you are and what you desire

- Help you gain clarity on your goals, aspirations, and dreams

- Identify aspects and issues of your life where you feel unhappy, unfulfilled, and want to change

- Gather key elements in preparation for evaluating your spaces during *The Feng Shui Consultation*

"If there is light in the soul
There will be beauty in the person.
If there is beauty in the person
There will be harmony in the house.
If there is harmony in the house
There will be order in the nation.
If there is order in the nation
There will be peace in the world."

– Chinese Proverb

Beginning Our Conversation

I want to really get to know you, and what you want to create in your life at this time. Please complete the following sentences.

1. My current goals and dreams are:

_____

_____

_____

2. My core values are:

_____

_____

_____

3. The most meaningful aspects of my life are:

_____

_____

_____

4. Areas of my life I want to change or improve are:

_____

_____

_____

5. My greatest personal gifts and talents are:

_____

_____

_____

6. What makes me truly happy is:

_____

_____

_____

7. My soul's purpose is:

_____

_____

_____

8. My reasons for requesting a Feng Shui consult are:

_____

_____

_____

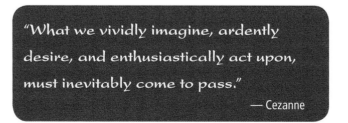

"What we vividly imagine, ardently
desire, and enthusiastically act upon,
must inevitably come to pass."

— Cezanne

23

Setting Priorities for Your Life Goals and Aspirations

together we complete this Personal Profile. The Profile represents the areas and issues of your life described as The Nine Life Aspirations. During *The Feng Shui Conversation*, I guide you to rank them from those that are out of balance to those that give you the most satisfaction.

Please place an X in the box that best indicates how you are currently feeling in these areas.

#1 Not satisfied with this area. Need help with issues. Reflects blocked energy and desire for change.

#5 All is well. Couldn't be better. No problems here. Reflects abundant energy and joyful flow at this moment.

Calculating the Results of Your Personal Profile.

Identify your Life Aspirations areas in Columns 1 and 2. These represent areas you wish to improve. Column 3 may be neutral. Areas marked in Columns 4 and 5 you find most satisfying. Then match areas in Column 1 and 2 with numbers in Column A, which represent areas of The Bagua. These are the aspects of your life ready for change, chi cultivation, and activation to create more happiness and balance in your life.

The Areas You Selected for Improvement in Your Life:

1. _____

2. _____

3. _____

4. _____

Your Personal Profile of the Nine Life Aspirations

A	B	The Nine Life Aspirations	1	2	3	4	5
3	1	Family Health					
3	2	Connection to Ancestors					
4	3	Wealth & Prosperity					
4	4	Cash Flow					
5	5	Mental Clarity					
5	6	Harmony & Balance					
6	7	Travel					
6	8	Benefactors & Support System					
6	9	How Much You Help Others					
7	10	Creative Expression, Creative Projects					
7	11	Your Children & Grandchildren					
8	12	Spiritual Life					
8	13	Wisdom, Knowledge, Intuition					
9	14	Fame & Reputation					
9	15	Recognition for Your Work					
1	16	Career Direction & Life's Journey					
1	17	Work Satisfaction					
2	18	Relationship with Self					
2	19	Family					
2	20	Friends					
2	21	Professional					
2	22	Love & Romance					
3	23	Your Physical Health					
3	24	Your Emotional Health					

Flourishing in Your Life

there is great wisdom in a song I learned in the Girl Scouts oh so many years ago, which began, "If you are happy and you know it, clap your hands!" Knowing how you really feel, whenever, wherever, however it may be, is about being in the present, being conscious, and owning your reality.

Long before our founding fathers wrote, "that all men are created equal, that they are endowed by their Creator with certain unalienable Rights, that among these are Life, Liberty, and the pursuit of Happiness," much has been written about attaining this often elusive state of being: Happiness.

Tal Ben-Shahar, in his book, *Happier,* defines happiness as "the overall experience of pleasure and meaning." Martin E.P. Seligman, a pioneer in the positive psychology movement, expanded his previous interpretation of happiness in *Authentic Happiness* to a theory of well-being in his book *Flourish*: "Well-being is a construct: and well-being, not happiness, is the topic of positive psychology. [It] has five measurable elements (PERMA) that count toward it: Positive emotion (of which happiness and life satisfaction are all aspects), Engagement, Relationships, Meaning and Achievement... The goal of positive psychology in well-being theory...is to increase the amount of flourishing in your own life and on the planet."

Seligman reports research of Felicia Huppert and Timothy So, who defined and measured flourishing in each of twenty-three European Union nations and added their definition: "to flourish, an individual must have all the 'core features' and three of the six 'additional features.'"

Were you to take a similar scale, how would you rate yourself?

I am Flourishing in My Life in the Following Ways

(#1) Represents low flourishing, (#5) Represents high flourishing
(*) Indicates PERMA – 5 core values, (+) Indicates additional features

*Positive Emotion	Taking all things together, how happy would you say you are?	1	2	3	4	5
*Engagement, *Interest	I love learning new things.	1	2	3	4	5
*Meaning, *Purpose	I generally feel that what I do in my life is valuable and worthwhile.	1	2	3	4	5
+Self-Esteem	I generally, feel very positive about myself.	1	2	3	4	5
+Optimism	I'm always optimistic about my life and future.	1	2	3	4	5
+Resilience	When things go wrong in my life, it generally doesn't take me a long time to get back to normal. (#5 indicates the most resilience.)	1	2	3	4	5
+Positive Relationships	There are people in my life who really care about me.	1	2	3	4	5
+Vitality	I approach my life tasks with energy and vigor.	1	2	3	4	5
+Self Determination	I pursue and complete my tasks with resolve and purpose.	1	2	3	4	5
+Positive Accomplishment (added by Seligman)	I take pleasure in my work and life accomplishments for their own sake.	1	2	3	4	5

Clarifying Life Goals

Selecting My Life Goals and Aspirations
for Feng Shui Activation and Remedy

My Goals and Intentions are as follows:

1. Career & Life's Journey _____

_____

_____

2. Love & Relationships _____

_____

_____

3. Health & Ancestors _____

_____

_____

4. Prosperity & Wealth_____

_____

_____

5. Harmony & Balance _____

_____

_____

6. Benefactors, Helpful People & Travel _____

_____

_____

7. Future Goals, Creative Projects & Children _____

_____

_____

8. Intuition, Wisdom, Spiritual Life_____

_____

_____

9. Fame & Reputation _____

_____

_____

The Bagua

You are now ready to identify areas of The Bagua that correspond to the areas you selected to alter or improve in your life. These are based on *The Feng Shui Conversation* and your *Feng Shui Profile of the Nine Life Aspirations*. Correlate your numbers in column A on page 25 with numbers in the boxes below. These are areas of your life you desire to shift and change leading to a happier life by making new placements with intention.

4	9	2
Wealth & Prosperity	**Fame & Reputation**	**Love & Relationships**
Purple	Red	Pink
WIND	FIRE	EARTH
Wood	Fire	Earth (Fertile)
3	**5**	**7**
Health & Ancestors	**Harmony & Balance**	**Creativity & Future Projects**
Green	Yellow	White
THUNDER	TAI CHI	LAKE
Wood	Earth	Metal
8	**1**	**6**
Wisdom & Spirituality	**Career & Life's Journey**	**Travel & Benefactors**
Blue	Black	Grey
MOUNTAIN	WATER	HEAVEN
Earth (mountain)	Water	Metal

Locating Your New Placements

Example for Locating New Placements

Assume that your three priority goals to change your life are Wisdom 8, Health 3, and Reputation 9. Then the areas of the Bagua for activation on your property, and in your rooms, would be as follows, duplicated in each location with a metaphorical remedy to suit your intended goals. The Bagua is overlaid from the mouth of chi.

Activation Areas of the Bagua as example

On Property
EXTERIOR Landscape Environment
Placement for Corrections and Remedies

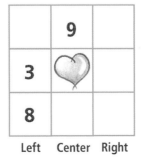

Left   Center   Right

DRIVEWAY ENTRANCE OPTIONS
MOUTH OF CHI

In Home

INTERIOR Landscape Environment
Placement for Corrections
and Remedies

Door   Door   Door
**FRONT DOOR ENTRANCE OPTIONS
MOUTH OF CHI**

In Bedroom

INTERIOR Landscape Environment
Placement for Corrections
and Remedies

Door   Door   Door
**BEDROOM DOOR OPTIONS
MOUTH OF CHI**

In Home Office

INTERIOR Landscape Environment
Placement for Corrections
and Remedies

Door   Door   Door
**OFFICE DOOR ENTRANCE OPTIONS
MOUTH OF CHI**

In Kitchen

INTERIOR Landscape Environment
Placement for Corrections
and Remedies

Door   Door   Door
**OFFICE DOOR ENTRANCE OPTIONS
MOUTH OF CHI**

Evaluating Landscape Features ©

The Ideal Feng Shui Site Creates the "Arm Chair Effect"

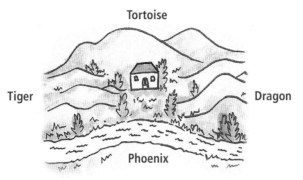

Tortoise

Tiger

Dragon

Phoenix

The Four Mystical Animals Create "The Arm Chair Effect"

Features of My Property and Exterior Landscape

My property is a complete shape.	1	2	3	4	5
I have a solid backing at the rear of my property. *(Tortoise)*	1	2	3	4	5
I am protected on the Right side of my property. *(Dragon-yang)*	1	2	3	4	5
I am protected on the Left side of my property. *(Tiger-yin)*	1	2	3	4	5
I have a distant view when I leave my front door. *(Phoenix)*	1	2	3	4	5
The entrance to my property is from a circular driveway.	1	2	3	4	5

Features of My Home and Interior Landscape

My home is a complete shape.	1	2	3	4	5
I have a sold backing at the rear of my house.	1	2	3	4	5
I have a solid backing wall behind my bed.	1	2	3	4	5
I have a solid headboard and footboard on my bed.	1	2	3	4	5
I have a solid desk chair with good backing.	1	2	3	4	5
I have a solid backing wall behind my desk chair.	1	2	3	4	5
I have a water feature in front of my house.	1	2	3	4	5
I am in good health, with energy and vitality.	1	2	3	4	5
I feel a sense of harmony and balance in my home.	1	2	3	4	5

Features of Home and Interior Landscape (cont.)

Structural elements interrupt the flow of chi.	1	2	3	4	5
I use the front door entrance to my home frequently.	1	2	3	4	5

I feel most comfortable in these rooms: _____

I feel most uncomfortable in these rooms: _____

Features of My Home Office or Workspace

I have a solid backing on the property where I work.	1	2	3	4	5
I have a solid backing in the building where I work.	1	2	3	4	5
I have a solid backing behind my desk chair.	1	2	3	4	5
I have solid desk chair with good backing.	1	2	3	4	5
I face the door when I sit at my desk chair.	1	2	3	4	5
I feel alert with vitality and energy while I work.	1	2	3	4	5

Features of My Bedroom

My Bedroom is a complete shape.	1	2	3	4	5
My bed has a headboard and a footboard.	1	2	3	4	5
My bed is not in line with the door.	1	2	3	4	5
My bed is set against a solid wall.	1	2	3	4	5

My Life Goals and Aspirations Are Being Met

Career, Work, Life Journey *(Water Energy)*	1	2	3	4	5
Relationship with Self, Family, Friends *(Earth Energy)*	1	2	3	4	5
Health, Vitality, Family Ancestry *(Wood Energy)*	1	2	3	4	5
Prosperity, Wealth, Cash Flow *(Wood Energy)*	1	2	3	4	5
Mental Health and Overall Balance *(Earth Energy)*	1	2	3	4	5
Benefactors, Helpful People, Travel *(Metal Energy)*	1	2	3	4	5
Creative, Future Projects, Children *(Metal Energy)*	1	2	3	4	5
Spiritual Life, Wisdom, Knowing *(Earth Energy)*	1	2	3	4	5
Reputation, Recognition for your Work *(Fire Energy)*	1	2	3	4	5
I Feel Happy, Healthy, Balanced, and Prosperous.	1	2	3	4	5

Having Fun with Chinese Astrology

Feng Shui encompasses a philosophy of environs as well as cosmology. It is based on the *I Ching* or *Book of Changes*, applying the balancing qualities of yin and yang incorporating divination and oracles. Not only does Feng Shui consider the ideal home site and environment but also how the proper timing for events and actions may affect your prosperity and destiny. Prior to your consultation, I request your birthday, month and year, to share a touch of your Chinese Astrology and to calculate your personal trigram for the best energetic colors for your personal spaces and your "lucky directions." Will your astrology ring true for you and your life?

> "To know Humanity, understand Earth.
>
> To know Earth, understand Heaven.
>
> To know Heaven, understand the Way.
>
> To know the Way, understand the great within yourself."
>
> — Tao Te Ching

Offering this Feng Shui Astrology at the Time of Your Consultation

Your Date of Birth, Month and Year	_____ _____ _____
Your Feng Shui Astrology Based on 9 Star Ki	Your Principal #_____ Your Character #_____ Your Destiny #_____
Birth Year Element and Color	_____ _____
Birth Year Animal and Color	_____ _____
Birth Year Animal Characteristics from Classic Chinese Almanac	Birth Year Characteristics and Birth Year Forecast
Personal Energy Trigram Element and Color	Fire, Earth, Metal, Water, Wood Red, Terra Cotta, Gold/Silver, Blue, or Green
Best Supportive Elements and Color	Red, Terra Cotta, Gold/Silver, Blue, or Green
Best Combinations of Colors for Bedroom and Office	Red, Terra Cotta, Gold/Silver, Blue or Green
Your Lucky Directions – East Group or West Group	East Group (Sitting in) N, S, E, SE or West Group (Sitting in) SW, NW, NE, W
House Numerology Your House has vibration of number ___.	Essence of home with vibration of number ___. Challenging Aspects of home with Vibration of number ___.
The Five Element Theory includes: Fire, Earth, Metal, Water, and Wood	Productive Cycle - Fire, Earth, Metal, Water, Wood Controlling Cycle - Metal, Wood, Earth, Water, Fire

Your Feng Shui Astrology

Nine Star Ki Astrology Based on Your Birth date

Nine Star Ki Astrology originated in China. Common sense principles and ancient science merged to form an astrological system based on a nine year cycle of the universe and how yin yang theory contribute to human transformation. Who are you? What is your essential character? How do you express yourself to the world? And then, where are you in the nine year cycle of life on earth?

For your Feng Shui astrology, I calculate your principal, character, and destiny numbers. I calculate how you flow annually through your nine year cycle. I have found that it does fit the larger picture of how clients are planning their lives to achieve the harmony and happiness they seek.

Below I use the flow of my Nine Star Ki numbers of 3.8.9 as an example. My principal number is 3. Space is left below for your Nine Star Ki numbers. Notice on the next page how the position of the numbers change and how I move from sprouting, to rapid growth, to fluctuation in 2013, in 2014, and in 2015.

3	8	9
Principal Number	Character Number	Destiny Number
WOOD Energy	EARTH Energy	FIRE Energy

"9 Star Ki Astrology offers you a set of tools to map your life and negotiate the challenges that lie ahead."

— Jon Sandifer

The Magic Square

4	9	2
3	5	7
8	1	6

The Energies of the Magic Square

4 Rapid Growth	9 Fame	2 Germination
3 Sprouting	5 Fluctuation	7 Celebration
8 Stillness	1 Planning	6 Prosperity

Nine Star Ki Feng Shui Astrology
The Annual Flow of a Person with Numbers 3.8.9

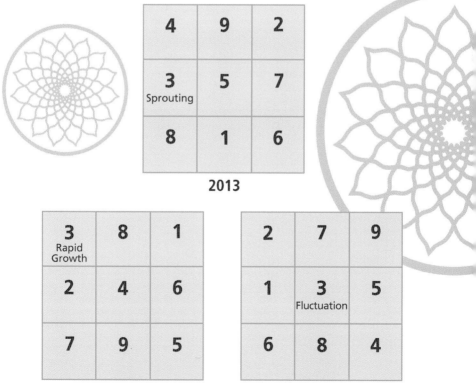

4	9	2
3 Sprouting	5	7
8	1	6

2013

3 Rapid Growth	8	1
2	4	6
7	9	5

2014

2	7	9
1	3 Fluctuation	5
6	8	4

2015

III–The Feng Shui Consultation

Now that we have completed *The Feng Shui Conversation*, and I understand your wishes to improve your life, we are ready to begin *The Feng Shui Conversation*. I will:

• Evaluate exterior and interior environments of your property, home, and rooms from the macro to the micro point of view

• Recommend adjustments to structure, shapes, symbols, and furniture arrangements to improve the flow of chi

• Suggest new placements known as cures and remedies as visual metaphors to implement your life goals and aspirations

• Teach you to activate and anchor your new placements with intention and ceremony

• Improve chi cultivation of your home, body, and life

• Foster health and vitality, harmony and balance, leading to happiness, success, and prosperity by sharing Feng Shui principles with you

"Go confidently
in the direction
of your dreams.
Live the life
you imagined."

—Thoreau

Honoring Your Process with Feng Shui

Levels of Chi Cultivation and Creating Your Success

Everything changes. Nature is our teacher. Often we wish our lives remained the same; at other times we embrace change and even seek it. If you are ready to take action on something you want in your life, such as a new job, different relationship, or deeper spiritual life, you can take the first step in your home. Set your deepest desires before you in a new arrangement, a personal "cure," using principles of Feng Shui, and make use of nature's gifts as much as possible. I suggest your process may be in stages similar to this:

You desire *Change.*
It takes *Courage* to transform your life.
Clarity is essential for beginning.

During The Feng Shui *Conversation,*
we refined your issues among the Nine Life Aspirations

- Health & Family
- Fame & Reputation
- Creative Projects & Children
- Career & Life's Journey
- Harmony & Balance

- Wealth & Prosperity
- Love & Relationships
- Helpful People & Travel
- Spiritual Life & Wisdom
- The Tai Chi

Now, during The Feng Shui Consultation, we will:

Critique and review your exterior and interior landscape and spaces,

Consider the clutter, Clean and Clear the energy,

Evaluate and Cultivate the Chi flow,

Find Cures, remedies, and solutions in order to

Create your new placements with intention,

Complete a Ceremony to activate and seal your cures, remedies, and reminders, and then,

Celebrate and appreciate your results.

Reviewing Key Placements

Correcting Imbalances and Attracting Blessings

Bed
Empowerment

Desk
Financial Success

Stove
Health and Vitality

Living Room Sofa
Welcoming Friends

Chi Flow Enters from the "Mouth of Chi"

Driveway Entrance

Front Door

Windows

Cosmic Chi

Having a Complete Shape for Property and Home Is Ideal

Property Shape

Home
Horizontal

Home
Vertical

Home with Missing Areas Affects Your Life and Body in Negative Ways

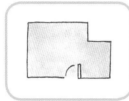

Missing Area in Relationships

Missing Area in Fame

Home with Enhanced Areas Affects Your Life and Body in Positive Ways

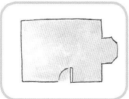

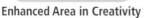

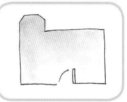

Enhanced Area in Creativity

Enhanced Area in Wealth

The Ideal Placement for Bed and Desk Face the Door but Are Not in Same Alignment

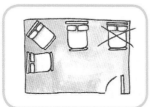

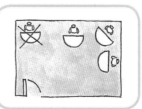

Ideal Placement for Bed

Ideal Placement for Desk

43

The Aspects of the Bagua

A Template for Placement
of the Feng Shui Energies
and the Nine Life Aspirations

4	9	2
Wealth & Prosperity	**Fame & Reputations**	**Love & Relationships**
Green, Purple, Red	Red	Red, Pink, White
WOOD (mature)	FIRE	EARTH (fertile)
Southeast	South	Southwest
Pelvis	Eye	Internal Organ
Eldest Daughter	Middle Daughter	Mother & Sister
WIND	FIRE	EARTH
Sun	Li	Kun
3	**5**	**7**
Health & Family	**Balance & Harmony**	**Creativity & Future Projects**
Green	Yellow	White
WOOD (Spring)	EARTH	METAL
East		West
Foot	Health	Mouth
Eldest Son	Tai Chi	Youngest Daughter
THUNDER		LAKE
Chen		Tui
8	**1**	**6**
Wisdom & Spirituality	**Career & Life Journey**	**Helpful People & Travel**
Green, Blue, Black	Black	Black, Grey, White
EARTH (mountain)	WATER	METAL
Northeast	North	Northwest
Hand	Ear	Head
Youngest Son	Middle Son	Father
MOUNTAIN	WATER	HEAVEN
Ken	Kan	Chien

Come Home to Yourself, Your Sacred Inner Space

Take time to be quiet, silent, and still.
Know calmness as much as you know activity.
In silence you hear your own voice and wisdom.
Intuition speaks in whispers as an angel on your shoulder.
Hush. Listen. Be still.
Breathe.

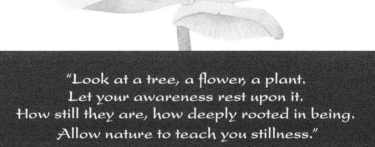

"Look at a tree, a flower, a plant.
Let your awareness rest upon it.
How still they are, how deeply rooted in being.
Allow nature to teach you stillness."

"We depend on nature not only for our physical survival.
We also need nature to show us the way home, the way
out of the prison of our own minds. We got lost in doing,
thinking, remembering, anticipating – lost in a maze of
complexity and a world of problems."

"We have forgotten what rocks, plants, and
animals still know.
We have forgotten how to *be* – to be still,
To be ourselves, to be where life is: Here and Now."

— Eckhart Tolle, *Stillness Speaks*

The Bagua

Template for New Placements and
Locating Feng Shui Energies
on Your

Property

Rear of Property

4 **Wealth &** **Prosperity** WOOD Green, Purple, Red	**9** **Reputation &** **Respect** FIRE Red	**2** **Relationships &** **Love** EARTH (fertile) Red, Pink, White
3 **Health &** **Family** WOOD Green	**5** **Balance &** **Harmony** EARTH Yellow	**7** **Creativity &** **Future Projects** METAL White
8 **Spirituality &** **Wisdom** EARTH (mountain) Green, Blue, Black	**1** **Career &** **Life Journey** WATER Black	**6** **Travel &** **Helpful People** METAL Black, Grey, White

Front of Property

DRIVEWAY	DRIVEWAY	DRIVEWAY

Evaluating Your Property through Feng Shui Eyes

I review influence of shape of property, road, street, bridges, pointed edges, trees, water features, transformers, telephone poles, placement of outbuildings, colors, topography, gardens, swimming pool, location and type of driveway entrance, neighboring properties, position of your home and outbuildings on the property, others.

 **Consultation Recommendations and Notes**

_____

_____

_____

_____

_____

_____

_____

_____

_____

_____

_____

_____

> "In Dwelling, live close to the ground. In thinking, keep to the simple. In conflict, be fair and generous. In governing don't try to control. In work, do what you enjoy. In family life, be completely present."
> — Lao Tzu

The Bagua

Template for New Placements and
Locating Feng Shui Energies
in Your

Home

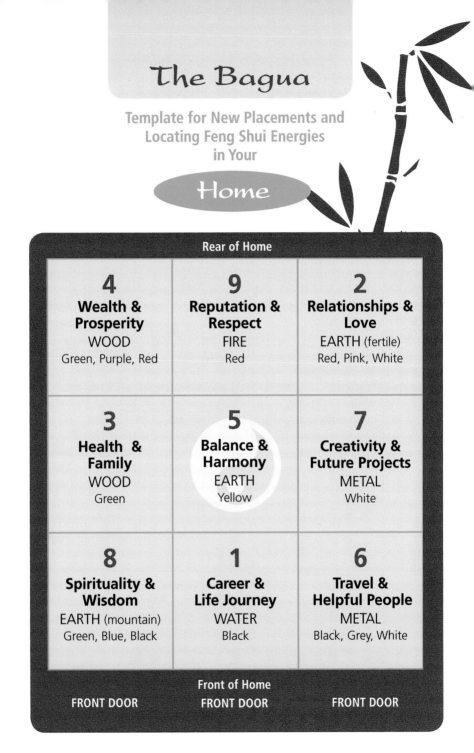

Rear of Home

4	9	2
Wealth & Prosperity	**Reputation & Respect**	**Relationships & Love**
WOOD	FIRE	EARTH (fertile)
Green, Purple, Red	Red	Red, Pink, White
3	5	7
Health & Family	**Balance & Harmony**	**Creativity & Future Projects**
WOOD	EARTH	METAL
Green	Yellow	White
8	1	6
Spirituality & Wisdom	**Career & Life Journey**	**Travel & Helpful People**
EARTH (mountain)	WATER	METAL
Green, Blue, Black	Black	Black, Grey, White

Front of Home

| FRONT DOOR | FRONT DOOR | FRONT DOOR |

Evaluating Your Home through Feng Shui Eyes

I review influence of shape of home and its position on property, structural elements, foyer, missing and enhanced areas, front door, backdoor alignment, master bedroom behind heart center, position of bed, desk, stove, living room sofa, beams, pillars, columns, slanted walls, ceilings, piercing arrows, hallways, doors, brightness, light, windows, colors, symbols, paintings, art objects, chi flow, clutter, balance of Five Elements of Fire, Earth, Metal, Water, and Wood, others.

 Consultation Recommendations and Notes

_____

_____

_____

_____

_____

_____

_____

_____

_____

The Human Body

Energetically Fills Entire Interior Space of Home

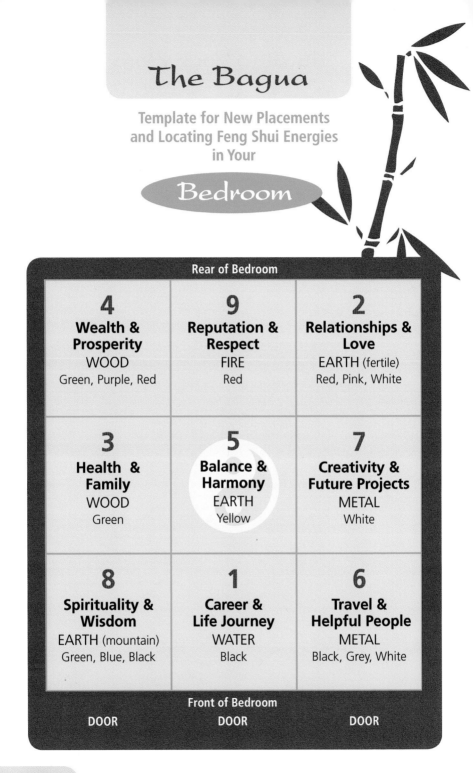

The Bagua

Template for New Placements
and Locating Feng Shui Energies
in Your

Bedroom

Rear of Bedroom		
4 **Wealth &** **Prosperity** WOOD Green, Purple, Red	**9** **Reputation &** **Respect** FIRE Red	**2** **Relationships &** **Love** EARTH (fertile) Red, Pink, White
3 **Health &** **Family** WOOD Green	**5** **Balance &** **Harmony** EARTH Yellow	**7** **Creativity &** **Future Projects** METAL White
8 **Spirituality &** **Wisdom** EARTH (mountain) Green, Blue, Black	**1** **Career &** **Life Journey** WATER Black	**6** **Travel &** **Helpful People** METAL Black, Grey, White
Front of Bedroom		
DOOR	DOOR	DOOR

Evaluating Your Bedroom through Feng Shui Eyes

I review influence of master bedroom placement in house, shape of bedroom, missing and enhanced areas, bed position, shape of headboard and footboard, position of children's bedrooms, chi flow, fresh air, electro-magnetic field, quality as personal space, features that affect relationship with self and others, color compatibility with personal element, paintings, objects, furniture placement, beams, pillars, columns, slanted walls, ceilings, piercing arrows, doors, brightness, light, windows, colors, symbols, paintings, art objects, chi flow, clutter, balance of Five Elements of Fire, Earth, Metal, Water, and Wood, others.

Consultation Recommendations and Notes

_____

_____

_____

_____

_____

_____

_____

_____

CHINESE SYMBOLS ARE RICH IN METAPHORS

Mandarin ducks mate for life.
A remedy for Love and Relationships

The Bagua

Template for New Placements
and Locating Feng Shui Energies
in Your

Children's Bedrooms

Rear of Room		
4 **Wealth &** **Prosperity** WOOD Green, Purple, Red	**9** **Reputation &** **Respect** FIRE Red	**2** **Relationships &** **Love** EARTH (fertile) Red, Pink, White
3 **Health &** **Family** WOOD Green	**5** **Balance &** **Harmony** EARTH Yellow	**7** **Creativity &** **Future Projects** METAL White
8 **Spirituality &** **Wisdom** EARTH (mountain) Green, Blue ,Black	**1** **Career &** **Life Journey** WATER Black	**6** **Travel &** **Helpful People** METAL Black, Grey, White
Front of Room		
DOOR	DOOR	DOOR

Evaluating Your Children's Bedrooms through Feng Shui Eyes

I review location of children's bed rooms in home, bed shape, style, size, and placement in room, structural elements, lighting, missing and enhanced areas, chi flow, fresh air, electro-magnetic field, furniture placement and design, yin yang factors, colors, textures, beams, pillars, slanted walls, ceilings, piercing arrows, clutter, organization, balance of the Five Elements of Fire, Earth, Metal, Water, and Wood, others.

 Consultation Recommendations and Notes

_____

_____

_____

_____

_____

_____

_____

_____

"The two most important days in our life are the day you are born . . . and the day you find out why."
— Mark Twain

"Twenty years from now you will be more disappointed by the things that you didn't do than by the ones you did do. So throw off the bowlines. Catch the trade winds in your sails. Explore. Dream. Discover."
— Mark Twain

The Bagua

Template for New Placements
and Locating Feng Shui Energies
in Your

Living Room

Rear of Room		
4 **Wealth &** **Prosperity** WOOD Green, Purple, Red	**9** **Reputation &** **Respect** FIRE Red	**2** **Relationships &** **Love** EARTH (fertile) Red, Pink, White
3 **Health &** **Family** WOOD Green	**5** **Balance &** **Harmony** EARTH Yellow	**7** **Creativity &** **Future Projects** METAL White
8 **Spirituality &** **Wisdom** EARTH (mountain) Green, Blue ,Black	**1** **Career &** **Life Journey** WATER Black	**6** **Travel &** **Helpful People** METAL Black, Grey, White
Front of Room		
DOOR	DOOR	DOOR

Evaluating Your Living Room through Feng Shui Eyes

I review front door entrance, foyer, and chi flow to Living Room, room shape, placement in home, placement of primary sofa and chairs, structural elements, lighting, enhanced areas and missing corners, furniture placement and design, yin yang factors, colors, textures, metaphor of art and objects, beams, pillars, slanted walls, ceilings, piercing arrows, clutter, balance of the Five Elements of Fire, Earth, Metal, Water, and Wood, others.

 Consultation Recommendations and Notes

_____

_____

_____

_____

_____

_____

_____

_____

_____

_____

_____

_____

_____

"Home is the place where character is built, where sacrifices to contribute to the happiness of others are made, and where love has taken up its abode."
— Elijah Kellogg

The Bagua

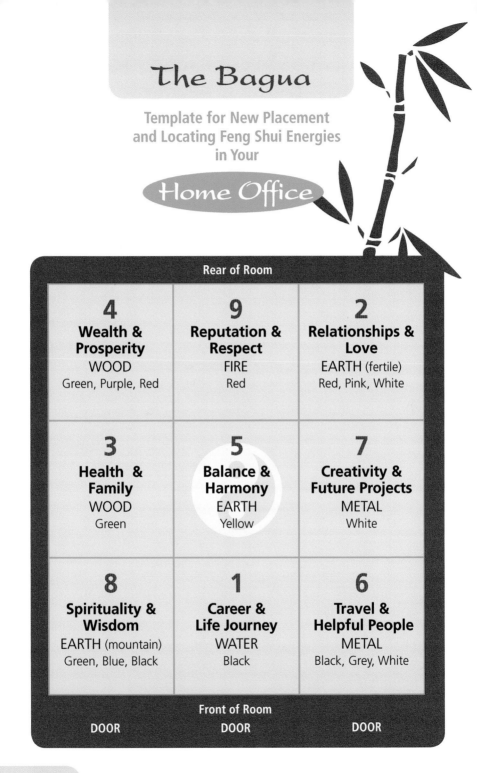

Template for New Placement
and Locating Feng Shui Energies
in Your

Home Office

Rear of Room

4	9	2
Wealth & Prosperity	**Reputation & Respect**	**Relationships & Love**
WOOD	FIRE	EARTH (fertile)
Green, Purple, Red	Red	Red, Pink, White
3	5	7
Health & Family	**Balance & Harmony**	**Creativity & Future Projects**
WOOD	EARTH	METAL
Green	Yellow	White
8	1	6
Spirituality & Wisdom	**Career & Life Journey**	**Travel & Helpful People**
EARTH (mountain)	WATER	METAL
Green, Blue, Black	Black	Black, Grey, White

Front of Room

DOOR	DOOR	DOOR

Evaluating Your Home Office through Feng Shui Eyes

Influence of position of home office in the home, shape of home office, missing and enhanced areas, position of desk with respect to door entrance, size of desk, quality of desk chair, chi flow, fresh air, color compatibility with personal element, paintings, objects, beams, pillars, columns, slanted walls, ceilings, piercing arrows, brightness, light quality, windows, colors, symbols, paintings, art objects, chi flow, clutter, balance of Five Elements of Fire, Earth, Metal, Water, and Wood, others.

 Consultation Recommendations and Notes

_____

_____

_____

_____

_____

_____

_____

_____

_____

_____

_____

> "The wisdom traditions tell us that we can afford to slow down, take a breather, turn inwards, to master ourselves is to arrive home, at the center of being – the universal mandala."
>
> — Lama Surya Das

The Bagua

Template for New Placements
and Locating Feng Shui Energies
in Your

Kitchen

Rear of Room		
4 **Wealth &** **Prosperity** WOOD Green, Red, Purple	**9** **Reputation &** **Respect** FIRE Red	**2** **Relationships &** **Love** EARTH (fertile) Red, Pink, White
3 **Health &** **Family** WOOD Green	**5** **Balance &** **Harmony** EARTH Yellow	**7** **Creativity &** **Future Projects** METAL White
8 **Spirituality &** **Wisdom** EARTH (mountain) Green, Black, Blue	**1** **Career &** **Life Journey** WATER Black	**6** **Travel &** **Helpful People** METAL Black, Grey, White
Front of Room		
DOOR	DOOR	DOOR

Evaluating Your Kitchen through Feng Shui Eyes

I review influence of kitchen position in home, shape of kitchen, position of stove in relationship to refrigerator and sink, cleanliness, dining area, shape of kitchen table, design features to support the cook, colors, balance of Five Elements of Fire, Earth, Metal, Water, and Wood, others.

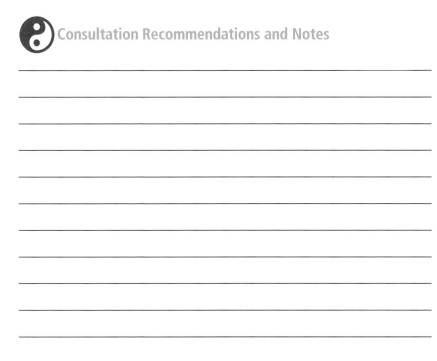

Consultation Recommendations and Notes

_____

_____

_____

_____

_____

_____

_____

_____

_____

_____

_____

"To the Human organism, there are two sources of Qi, breath and food."

"Feng Shui holds the (second) most important room in the house is the kitchen, where the preparation of food determines health – and hence the wealth – of all the house's occupants."

— Elizabeth Miles

Taking Time to Summarize Corrections

rior to implementing your suggested Feng Shui corrections, remedies, and reminders, let's take a moment to review them. New possibilities await.

Areas of your life you wish to improve or change:

1. _____
2. _____
3. _____

Corrections for your property and exterior environment:

1. _____
2. _____
3. _____

Corrections for your home and interior environment:

1. _____
2. _____
3. _____

Corrections for your bedroom:

1. _____
2. _____
3. _____

Corrections for your home office:

1. _____
2. _____
3. _____

Corrections for your living room:

1. _____
2. _____
3. _____

Corrections for your kitchen:

1. _____
2. _____
3. _____

"Life is a series of natural and spontaneous changes. Don't resist them - that only creates sorrow. Let reality be reality. Let things flow naturally forward in whatever way they like."
— Lao Tzu

IV–Taking Action to Create a Happier Life

Now you are ready to take action on your goals and dreams within your own sacred space of home when you:

- Consider the principles of Feng Shui based on centuries of observation of how landscape and home site contribute to happiness, success, and prosperity

- Embrace the synergy between ancient wisdom of Feng Shui, and modem, scientific research on well-being and happiness

- Take action steps beginning with clearing clutter

- Make suggested corrections to improve the flow of chi, create new placements with intention as metaphors for desired goals, and then seal changes with a ceremony

- Choose to begin new patterns that make you happy

"Taking charge of one's home or office environment — throwing out the excess, redecorating to one's taste, making it personal and psychologically comfortable, – could be the first step in reordering one's life."
—Mihaly Csikszentmihaly

Taking Action with Feng Shui

Create Visual Metaphors as Remedies

Feng Shui principles suggest you make a minimum of three changes in placement within three days or move twenty-seven items at one time with intention. Making immediate changes in your environment allows you to experience optimum results from your consultation. With your permission, we may have decided to rearrange some things and make changes during your consultation process.

For example, if your primary goal is to improve your Relationship with a partner, then you will make three new placements with intention. Place a remedy in each of the Relationship areas on your property, home, and bedroom (Earth gua 2). For a powerful shift in your relationship, place the bed against a solid wall, but not in alignment with the door. Having a solid headboard and footboard is most desirable. Placing your bed on a diagonal is a very dynamic option. And, should you wish to create or establish a new direction for your Career, focus on three new placements in Career, on the property, home, and bedroom (Water gua 1). Together we will select the most meaningful remedy, making creative use of the personal items that best symbolize your intentions. Like an acupuncturist's needle, you will draw energy and focus to that which you see every day. Your remedies act as daily reminders. "What you see is what you get."

We have everything we need. Feng Shui allows you to place your belongings in the proper position to enhance the goals you desire. Enjoy using your own objects, paintings, and treasures, to act as the metaphor you desire for your life and for your soul's purpose. Feng Shui with Lurrae is therapeutic, as it may quickly lead to a new sense of well-being. It is decorating with a twist. It employs ancient wisdom combined with your own creativity and design aesthetic to set the stage for a new life story.

Designing Your Own Remedies and Solutions

Correct Imbalances and Attract Blessings

Match your new placement and intention with one of the traditional Feng Shui cures and remedies, incorporating objects you love. Have fun using your special and meaningful belongings. Where appropriate select from the traditional Chinese Feng Shui cures below and combine with your own solutions. Be imaginative. Be playful. Go wild. It's your life.

Basic Feng Shui Cures and Remedies

COLOR Invites, enhances, or softens chi (eight trigram colors, seven colors of rainbow)

LIGHTS, BRIGHT OBJECTS: Lights up & expands chi (man-made crystal, candle, lantern)

SOUND: Keeps things moving (wind chime, music, bell, musical Instrument)

MOVING OBJECTS: Disperses & circulates negative chi (flag, mobile, sculpture, weather vane)

LIFE FORCE: Stimulates chi (live plant, bird, flower, fish, bonsai tree, pet, silk plants, flowers)

HEAVY OBJECTS: Diffuses fast energy & holds down (rock, statue, sculpture, yu bowl with 9 rocks inside)

POWER OBJECTS: Conveys strength & power (firecrackers ward off negative chi, arrowhead is power object, talisman is spiritual protection)

MIRRORS: Heals negative energy (Baqua mirror deflects negative chi, convex expands narrow places, concave turns negative upside down)

WATER FEATURES: Activates wealth (indoor & outdoor fountain, fish tank, brook, stream, pond with gold fish, vase, bowl of water)

FRAGRANCE & AROMATHERAPY: Clears negative chi (perfume, potpourri, incense, candles)

TRANSCENDENTAL CURES: Expands on basic cures (bamboo flute & fan lift oppressive chi, beaded curtain & screens act as divider, crystal & gem stones raise energy & vibration level)

OTHER: Assemblages created by your imagination and ingenuity or one that combines the Five Elements of Fire, Earth, Metal, Water, and Wood.

Choosing to Change Your Life

Here are examples of possible new placements for a person who has goals to improve Health (Wood 3), Spirituality (Earth 8), and Reputation (Fire 9). After making each placement, create a ceremony to seal your intentions. Remember to orient the Bagua over the mouth of chi of Property, Home, and Bedroom.

Bagua Template for Property, Home, and Bedroom

4	9	2
3	5	7
8	1	6

Mouth of Chi Options

On the Property

HEALTH & FAMILY (GUA 3): Plant a tree or three lush green plants such as hosta, as a symbol of abundant health and a united family.

SPIRITUALITY & WISDOM (GUA 8): Build a cairn, a small stone tower, as a symbol to ground your own strong beliefs, wisdom, and intuition.

FAME & REPUTATION (GUA 9): Place a red sculpture or assemblage with Fire energy, such as twisted vines around red posts, to represent the triangular upward movement of flames and a growing reputation.

In Your Home

HEALTH & FAMILY (GUA 3): Place pictures of loved ones, three or nine new healthy green plants, lucky bamboo, or an arrangement of items made of wood that is beautiful and meaningful to you.

SPIRITUALITY & WISDOM (GUA 8): Create an assemblage or altar of objects and pictures symbolic of your personal beliefs.

FAME & REPUTATION (GUA 9): Paint your front door red to invite more chi to enter. Use your fireplace especially if in Gau 9 as the remedy. Embellish with symbols meaningful to your goal, such as a draft of a book, awards, and place within a red binder.

In Your Bedroom or Office

HEALTH & FAMILY (GUA 3): Be certain your bed is against a solid wall, with a headboard, and facing the door but not in the same alignment. Place a family picture on wall or a new healthy plant that is cared for, as you will now take better care of yourself.

SPIRITUALITY & WISDOM (GUA 8): Here you may use your most personal reminders of books, objects, and gratitude journal.

FAME & REPUTATION (GUA 9): Create metaphors using red. Frame your diplomas and honors with a red mat.

Create New Daily Habits that Make You Happy

HEALTH & FAMILY: Change your diet, increase exercise, start yoga.

SPIRITUALITY & WISDOM: Start a daily gratitude journal, meditate ten minutes daily in your quiet space, walk in the woods. Spend time appreciating the results you created from your new rituals.

FAME & REPUTATION: Wear red and brighter colors, smile, be compassionate, show appreciation, serve others, express your love.

> "Watch your thoughts; They become words.
> Watch your words; They become actions.
> Watch your actions: They become habits.
> Watch your habits; They become character.
> Watch your character; It becomes your destiny."
>
> — Lao Tzu

Designing
the Ceremony

A ceremony infuses a unique moment in time with meaning, such as marking the celebration of a birth, wedding, or special occasion. When the ceremonial action is accompanied by the spoken word, adding a hand or foot gesture, such as the breaking of glass at a Jewish wedding, it becomes symbolic. One may simply speak the desired outcome as a prayer, or select words that have a personal meaning for you.

Tibetan Tantric Buddhism Black Sect Feng Shui, taught by Master Lin Yun, suggests a ceremony called the Three Secrets Reinforcement for activations of the remedy while speaking the words, *Om Ma Ni Pad Me Hum* with a hand mudra. Professor Jes T.Y. Lim teaches the cure is best anchored and then sealed with a transcendental method.

Feng Shui ceremonies may combine aspects of the physical world with the transcendental and mystical, the concepts of sying and yi. Creating the time, space, and moment for a ceremony is an important aspect of activating your remedy and may be designed with words, affirmations, and actions most personal to you.

> "The way chi carries and fills our bodies indicates
> our health and destiny, not to mention how we
> interact in society, how we affect others and our
> immediate surroundings. Therefore, one's chi
> influences self, others, society and the universe."
>
> —Master Professor Lin Yun

Sequence for Designing Your Ceremonial Activations

- Set intention for your life and your desired outcome. Be specific.

- Identify appropriate "*Gua*" on your property, in your home, and in your bedroom.

- Select your remedy or cure, and make a new placement within three days.

- Activate with spoken words of intention, or a prayer of symbolic language such as, "The Three Secrets Reinforcement" from the practice of Tibetan Tantric Buddhism, Black Sect Feng Shui with the words, *Om Ma Ni Pad Me Hum* and a hand gesture.

- Repeat the above in each of the three areas of the Bagua of Property, Home, and Bedroom that represent the life aspiration and goal you seek. The Living Room, Kitchen, and Home Office may also be relevant for you.

- Different remedies may apply in each of the three *Guas*.

- Use your personal belongings to match your intention to the quality of the remedy. Use nature's bounty and objects where appropriate.

- Have fun. Use your creativity and imagination.

The Red Envelope Tradition

This ritual is deeply rooted in Chinese culture, as red envelopes are used to exchange money on auspicious occasions. Using the Red Envelope Tradition for a Feng Shui consultation honors the exchange of sacred knowledge and wisdom that has been passed down orally for generations from teacher to pupil and, now, between you and me. Giving red envelopes is a powerful symbol of exchange with many layers of meaning from ancient Chinese culture. Placing money in the red envelope demonstrates your respect for the sacred Feng Shui knowledge. It is an action that seals the intentions of the consultation. Some cash is suggested to invite a swift result.

The use of the red envelope also acts as a protection for the consultant who is sharing this ancient knowledge responsibly and respectfully. It separates the energy and karma between the consultant and client. When you take the time and effort to create or find red envelopes, it is another layer of honoring the ancient and sacred wisdom along with the transcendental quality of some of the cures. Red is associated with the life force energy and vibrates at a high frequency, symbolizing auspicious good luck, blessings, and power. I provide a red envelope to receive the fee should you not have one available.

Fees for Your Feng Shui Consultation

My Feng Shui Consultation fees are available upon request. They are based on the size of your property, out buildings, square feet of your home, and your expressed needs. Feng Shui Consultations for Business and Corporate Office are best performed after the completion of your Feng Shui Consultation of Home as the foundation for your Feng Shui environment.

Setting Your Follow-up Appointment

I suggest a follow-up consultation within the first three months of your initial consultation. I offer follow-up counseling and life coaching by phone or Skype as Conversations with Lurrae.

Welcoming Your Referrals and Testimonials

Do you know someone who might enjoy and benefit from a Feng Shui with Lurrae consultation? I offer a unique form of counseling and life coaching that takes place in personal spaces of home and business. Using home as the template, taking immediate action on designing your life enables you to realize joy, empowerment, and results more quickly toward your dreams and aspirations. Every chapter of life offers its particular challenges: young people transitioning toward adulthood in college or work, moving to a new home, looking for love, marriage or divorce, career changes, an empty nester, setting up a new business, or the death of a loved one. Nearly everyone may find applying the principles and ancient wisdom of Feng Shui helpful.

I appreciate and value feedback on my consultations. You may post a testimonial on my website, *FengShuiwithLurrae.com*. All consultations are confidential.

Sharing Feng Shui Stories

⚊ **HOME BUSINESS** *Dale moved her desk from where she sat under a basement window with her back to the door. She spent much of her day in a room with poor lighting devoid of fresh air. During her Consultation, Dale boldly made immediate changes to her space and her life. She moved her office to the first floor and transformed her living room into her office space, receiving the benefit of the fresh air and good chi from her garden. Her former dining room now became a combination living room and dining room. She married the man who came to dinner the evening after our consultation, as we had set the new position of her dining table for romance with heirloom china.*

⚊ **TEEN SHUI** *Sally is a talented young thirteen-year-old who wanted to prepare for her high school years and going to a boarding school. She placed her bed in a power position, revised her desk to the commanding position facing the door, and painted her ceiling gold, which inspired her to reach her high goals and golden dreams.*

⚊ **RELATIONSHIPS** *Janice rearranged her entire bedroom layout and placed her bed on a dynamic diagonal. She soon invited love and friendship into her life in ways she had only dreamed of and enhanced her front door entrance and garden spaces to activate her other life goals of spirituality, prosperity, and relationship with assemblages of great ingenuity and creativity using organic materials and memorabilia.*

FAMILY HARMONY *Simone started a home-based business but needed a space of her own. The large living room was rarely used. She moved her computer desk to a space in the living room with her desk chair facing the front door. She reconfigured the other section of the living room with couches and a large low coffee table retrieved from the basement set close to the fireplace. She found a place for her home business and the family enjoyed more fun and togetherness, playing games and engaging in conversation.*

RECENTLY DIVORCED *Marcy wanted to create a new independent life. She reconfigured her entire apartment with a new placement of bed, living room, and front door entrance to welcome her new life. Her kitchen and dining room design were most important to her as she loved to cook and wanted substantial seating for large family gatherings. Every room was an expression of intention to create a home very welcoming for family and friends to visit.*

LAW OFFICE *Legal partners occupied a new office space. They painted the front door red and hung a new brass light fixture near the outside entrance to attract new clientele. They situated their offices in the Fame and Relationship area of the building. They placed their personal desks in the power position on a dynamic diagonal facing the door of the office. Their solid wooden desks had no sharp corners to affect the clients. Their individual offices were decorated in colors compatible with their personal Trigram energy. Completed files were placed in the Wealth Corner of the building as the symbolic Treasure Chest. All paralegal desks were appropriately situated facing the office door. Clients were welcomed by a curved reception desk and consultations occurred at a round conference table. Their property has excellent features compatible with an ideal Feng Shui site. The stage was set for more success in business.*

Having Fun with Feng Shui

Some things you just can't explain. I call it the whisper of angels on your shoulder. It is your inner voice, the gut feeling — Intuition, the wisest knowing we have. When I follow it, I am on my path. When I don't, always in hindsight, I regret that I didn't listen to myself, didn't pay attention to the clues. The Universe always drops them for our eyes to see or our gut to feel, if we only pay enough attention.

And so it was when I was led to take my first weekend workshop in Feng Shui in Florida in 1995. My teacher was a disciple of Master Lin Yun. Within the first twenty minutes of the class, I knew I wanted to become a Feng Shui Consultant. It combined my knack for decorating, my background in therapeutic counseling, and my attraction to Buddhism and Chinese culture.

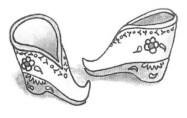

Early on, my father was fascinated by my new endeavor when he saw me returning from consultations with Red Envelopes. He said to me "What is this Fun Schway? If I had known you were interested in this, I would have bound your feet as a little girl." The Chinese shoes are in his memory and symbolic of following my path. What path are you called to follow in your life?

My intention is to bring happy chi and "fun shui" to your home or business, with reverence for the sacredness of being in your home and the meaning it holds for you. It is you. Your home represents all that you are and wish to be.

Life is a journey of many challenges and transitions. What happens is what you least expect and can never imagine. May your life be rich in glorious experiences and include frequent laughter that infuses your body and soul and keeps a smile on your face.

Enjoying Life's Journey

Ithaca

When you start on your journey to Ithaca,
then pray that the road is long,
full of adventure, full of knowledge.

Do not fear the Lestrygonians
and the Cyclops and the angry Poseidon.
You will never meet such as these on your path,
If your thoughts remain lofty, if a fine
emotion touches your body and your spirit.

You will never meet the Lestrygonians,
the Cyclops and the fierce Poseidon,
if you do not carry them within your soul,
if your soul does not raise them up before you.

Then pray that the road is long.
That the summer mornings are many,
that you will enter ports seen for the first time
with such pleasure, with such joy!

Stop at Phoenician markets,
and purchase fine merchandise,
mother-of-pearl and corals, amber and ebony,
and pleasurable perfumes of all kinds,
buy as many pleasurable perfumes as you can;
visit hosts of Egyptian cities,
to learn and learn from those who have knowledge.

Always keep Ithaca fixed in your mind.
To arrive there is your ultimate goal.
But do not hurry the voyage at all.
It is better to let it last for long years;
and even to anchor at the isle when you are old,
rich with all that you have gained on the way
not expecting that Ithaca will offer you riches.

Ithaca has given you the beautiful voyage.
Without her you would never have taken the road.
But she has nothing more to give you.

And if you find her poor, Ithaca has not defrauded you.
With the great wisdom you have gained, with so much experience,
You must surely have understood by then what Ithaca means.

— by Constantine Cavafy

> The author
> of this poem,
> Constantine
> Cavafy was
> born in 1863
> in Alexandria,
> Egypt to
> Greek parents.
>
> What paths
> will you select
> for your life's
> journey to design
> and create the
> life you desire?

Concluding Thoughts

I have always been attracted to the beauty of the lotus flower. It inspires me. Lotus flowers express strength and possibility. As a metaphor, they illustrate–no matter the situation–that it is possible for each person to live, overcome difficult circumstances, and flourish. The lotus flower is born in water, grows in mud and muck, yet rises up above water in all its beauty. It is poised on a single, straight, strong stem, unsoiled as the leaf is designed to allow water and debris to fall away.

So too, we are each beautiful and unique, singular and strong, and are capable of achieving whatever we desire. It's time to allow our fears and reservations to fall away, let go, and embrace the happiness we seek. We may design our lives using the principles of Feng Shui. We may begin with physical and energetic clearings and cleansing, gain clarity of purpose as to our goals, then anchor our intentions with new placements in our environments, and appreciate and celebrate the goals and dreams that we have achieved.

Our homes are a sacred space. Our energetic body fills our spaces in the same way an egg fills its shell. Our spaces offer powerful places where we may manifest our dreams. By making new placements with intention that symbolize our dreams, improving the flow and cultivation of chi, and by creating beneficial habits, we affect our own "inner spaces," realize happiness, and can change our lives. Let it be so for you. If not now, when?

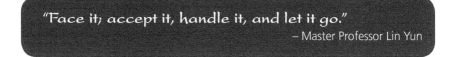

"Face it; accept it, handle it, and let it go."
– Master Professor Lin Yun

Manifesting Happiness & Flow

The Tangible and the Intangible

Feng Shui honors the realms of "sying and yi."
Sying is the tangible, physical, observable world,
Yi is the intangible, spiritual, and transcendental realm.

Call on your angels, spirit guides, and ancestors to participate with you, as you transform your intentions into reality.

Some people pursue happiness, others create it. As a gardener, plant seeds of change for greater well-being. Experience more joyful flow, meaning, and success.

Invite the universe to participate in the flowering of the seed dreams you have just created in your spaces.

Begin.

> " If I am not for myself, who will be for me?
> And if I am only for myself, what am I?
> And if not now, when? "
>
> – R.Hillel

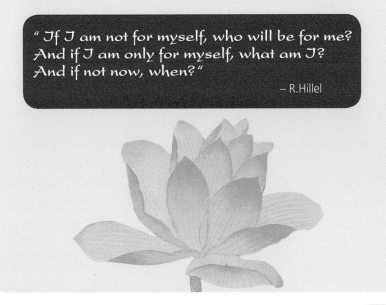

Defining
Feng Shui Terms

The Bagua An octagonal symbol of eight trigrams of the *I Ching*, ascribing eight characteristics relating to nature, man, family relationships, and areas of the home. The octagon may be superimposed on a property, home, or room from the vantage of the entrance to diagnose how the environment is affecting residents and to cure the problems.

Chi The cosmic breath or energy of atmosphere, earth, and humans. The most important principle of Feng Shui is to alter, enhance, correct, or improve human chi to increase health and vitality to achieve happiness, wealth, and success in life. Positive chi is sheng chi, negative chi is sha chi. Also known as Qi.

Cures and Remedies Feng Shui term to describe the corrections to chi flow to achieve a harmonic design, or to anchor an intention with a new placement, acting as the metaphor for a goal of the client.

Chu-shr Transcendental and illogical cures, the yet to be discovered, which lies outside science and range of knowledge.

Feng Shui Translated as "wind and water," it is the Chinese art and science of placement and design to balance and enhance exterior and interior environments and landscapes. A lost environmental science once only known to ancient civilizations as protected and sacred knowledge.

I Ching The mother of Chinese thought is expressed in this early mystical text of divination used to tell fortunes and offer guidance. The text offers wisdom depicting man's fate in constant flux. Its 64 trigrams, combinations of yin and yang symbols, provide a mystical chart where human fate is directly linked to surroundings and nature.

Ming Tang The number and levels of topography to reach a distant view. The first ming tang begins with the foyer and then looking out from the front door landing. Most desirable is a 180 degree view where the number of levels of Ming Tang count nine and beneficial when includes a water feature in front of the home.

Mouth of Chi The source of cosmic chi where it enters the property by driveway, home by front door, and rooms by individual doorways.

Om Ma Ni Pad Me Hum "The Jewel in the Lotus" is known as the Six True Words and the universal mantra of love and compassion, *Om – Ma – Ni – Pad – Me – Hum*. The corresponding colors of the Six True Words are White, Red, Yellow, Green, Blue, and Black.

Poison Arrows Negative energy directed to a person from a sharp angle created by two walls meeting, such as the corner of a building or sharp edge of furniture, such as a night stand. Most harmful when person is subjected to this angle for long periods of time as when in bed or at a desk.

Sying The physical world of forms and inherent aspect of Feng Shui. What is seen, observable, and understood, ranging from earth shapes, landscape, road directions, houses, and furniture placement.

The Tao "The Way," a philosophical concept of the unity of opposing opposites, yin and yang, that describes the true nature and harmonious governing principles of man and the universe. The goal is to live in harmony with the rhythms and flow of nature.

Taoism Both a philosophy and a religion, it preaches transcendence of the mundane through identifying with the Tao and laws of nature. As a religion, it integrates Chinese custom and wisdom, encompassing folklore, astrology, herbal medicine, and Feng Shui to help followers achieve worldly success and happiness.

Yi The intuitive, unobservable, transcendental world of the intentions and wishes of Feng Shui. It incorporates blessings, meditation, and ceremonies to strengthen and activate the practical, sying cures, and to adjust and alter chi from negative chi (sha chi) to positive chi (sheng chi).

Ying Yang Theory The Taoist concept that unites all polar opposites and causes harmony and balance in nature.

References

Anthony, Carol K. *A Guide to the I Ching.* Stowe: Anthony Publishing Company, 1981.
—. *The Philosophy of the I Ching.* Stowe: Anthony Publishing Company, 1981.

Ben-Shahar, Tal. *Happier: Learn the Secrets to Daily Joy and Lasting Fulfillment.* New York: McGraw Hill, 2007.

Butler, Jill. *Create the Space You Deserve: An Artistic Journey to Expressing Yourself Through Your Home.* Guilford: Globe Pequot Press, 2008.

Csikszentmihalyi, Mihaly. *Finding Flow: The Psychology of Engagement with Everyday Life.* New York: Basic Books, 1997.

Das, Lama Surya. *Awakening the Buddha Within.* New York: Broadway Books, 1997.

Hillel, Rabbi. *Pirkei Avot. Ethics of the Fathers.* New York: Merkos L'Inyonei Chinuch, 2005

Lewin, Roger. *Making Waves: Irving Dardik and his Superwave Principle.* New York: Rodale, 2005.

Lim, Jes T. Y. *Feng Shui & Your Health: A Guide to High Vitality.* Singapore: Times Books International, 1999
—. *Feng Shui for Office and Business.* Munich: GmbH & Co, KG, 2000.

Lin, Denise. *Sacred Space: Clearing and Enhancing the Energy of Your Home.* New York: Ballantine Books, 1996.

Lupone, Lurrae. "Feng Shui as Metaphor." *The Feng Shui Guild Newsletter,* March, 1997.
—. "Feng Shui: Honoring the Sacredness of Space." *Encyclopedia of Complementary Health Practice,* New York: Springer Publishing, 1999.
—. "Feng Shui: Therapy for the New Millennium." *Alternate Health Practitioner,* New York: Springer Publishing Co., 1999.

Miles, Elizabeth. *The Feng Shui Cookbook.* Secaucus: Carol Publishing Group, 1998.

Rossbach, Sarah. *The Chinese Art of Placement.* New York: Arkana, 1983.
—. *Interior Design with Feng Shui.* New York: Arkana, 1987.

Sandifer, Jon. *Feng Shui Astrology: Using 9 Star Ki to Achieve Harmony & Happiness in Your Life.* New York: Ballantine Publishing, 1997.

Seligman, Martin E.P. *Flourish: A Visionary New Understanding of Happiness and Well-being.* New York: Free Press, 2011.

Spear, William. *Feng Shui Made Easy: Designing Your Life with the Ancient Art of Placement.* New York: HarperCollins, 1995.

Sung, Dr. Edgar. *Classic Chinese Almanac.* San Francisco: MJE Publishing, 2012.

Tolle, Eckhart. *Stillness Speaks.* Vancouver: Namaste Publishing, 2003.

In Gratitude

I am forever grateful for the many people who have crossed my path, particularly my girlfriends from childhood to present day. They have enriched my life as we have listened, helped, and shared our journey with each other in ways only women seem to be able to do.

Lara Asher, for delightful and insightful editorial assistance.

Carollanne Crichton, Solavedi.com, for astrology readings.

Irving Dardik, Dardik-Institute.org, for creating the Superwave Theory, and LifeWaves exercise program for health, vitality, and longevity based on heart rate variability.

Trevor Dardik, LifeWaves.com, for personal training in LifeWaves exercise cycles.

Linda DiFazio, for friendship, travels and endless laughter.

Sara Garment, in loving memory for her counsel and friendship.

Girl Scouts of America, for lessons of living a life "in thought, word and deed" and "to always leave the campsite better than you found it."

Leslie Goldman, Your Enchanted Gardener. Plant Your Dream! Blog. CureZone.com, for lessons of planting "seed dreams," and his example of living and walking an authentic life with courage and passion.

Nora Hooper, NoraHooper.com, for intuitive readings.

Paul Halagan and Eileen Hine, HalaganDesign.com, for their beautiful and creative book design, and being so helpful and patient with opening up yet another path for me.

Silvio and Yetta Lupone, for the gift of life.

Marc and Jonathan Meyers, for the gift and joy of motherhood and becoming a grandmother.

Melodie Provenzano, MelodieProvenzano.com, for friendship, her playful illustrations and original drawing of the Feng Shui Fairy Godmother.

Juice Plus+®, for my health and daily dose of fruits, vegetables, and berries. LurraeLovesJuicePlus.com, Lurrae.TowerGarden.com.

ShenYun2013.com, ShenYunPerformingArts.org, for reviving 5,000 years of Chinese culture and civilization.

My spiritual teachers, and teachers of the ancient art and science of Feng Shui.

About the Author

Lurrae Lupone received her BA in Psychology and Elementary Education at the American University in Washington, DC and her MEd in Counseling and Guidance at Northeastern University in Boston, MA.

Her professional background includes work as an elementary school teacher, followed by group and individual counseling in social service agencies with unwed mothers, adolescent incarcerated youth, and in an outpatient drug addiction clinic of Boston City Hospital and The Manpower Development Training Program of New York City.

Lurrae was a licensed Realtor in Westchester County, New York and Connecticut, specializing in residential real estate, land sales, and new construction for twenty years.

Lurrae attended the Sarasota School of Massage Therapy and became a licensed massage therapist with a specialty in the ancient massage techniques of Thailand.

Her extensive Feng Shui Studies began in 1995 at the Institute for Bau-Biology and Ecology in Clearwater, Florida, followed by a Consultant Certificate from Metropolitan Institute for Feng Shui Studies. She attended the 1st, 2nd, and 3rd Feng Shui Conferences in California and seminars with master teacher Prof. Jes T.Y. Lim for Feng Shui Consultant Certifications. She attended the World Feng Shui Conference in Innsbruck, Austria in 2000.

Lurrae received several Consultant Certificates for Health and Vitality and for Business from QI-MAG International Feng Shui & Geobiology Institute in Heiden, Switzerland and Munich, Germany.

She has studied with Master Professor Lin Yun, Master Yap Jeng Hai, Lillian Too, Dr. Jes T.Y. Lim, Denise Lin, Karen Kingston, William Spear, and others.

Lurrae is a CIPP2 candidate, Certificate in Positive Psychology, at Kripalu, Lenox, MA., taught by Tal Ben-Shahar, Ph.D.

Lurrae has published several articles, including: Feng Shui: Therapy for the New Millennium, Feng Shui: Honoring the Sacredness of Space, and Feng Shui: Life as Metaphor.

Lurrae is a life coach, teacher, and speaker on Feng Shui. This is her first book.